Extreme Weather (Tornadoes To Hurricanes)

Speedy Publishing LLC
40 E. Main St. #1156
Newark, DE 19711

www.speedypublishing.com

Copyright 2014
9781635011050
First Printed October 24, 2014

All Rights reserved. No part of this book may be reproduced or used in any way or form or by any means whether electronic or mechanical, this means that you cannot record or photocopy any material ideas or tips that are provided in this book.

Extreme Weather Facts...

Hurricanes, tornadoes and typhoons usually form in tropical areas of the world. Hurricanes develop over warm water and use it as an energy source.

How Hurricanes, tornadoes and typhoons are formed:

1. Hurricanes form over a large mass of warm ocean water during the warmer months.

2. Air from surrounding areas with higher air pressure pushes in to the low pressure area.

3. Then that "new" air becomes warm and moist and rises, too.

4. As the warm air continues to rise, the surrounding air swirls in to take its place.

5. As the warmed, moist air rises and cools off, the water in the air forms clouds.

6. The whole system of clouds and wind spins and grows, fed by the ocean's heat and water evaporating from the surface.

7. This produces strong gusty winds, heavy rain and thunderclouds that is called a tropical disturbance.

8. As the air pressure drops and there are sustained winds up to 38 miles per hour, it is called a tropical depression.

9. When the cyclonic winds have sustained speeds from 39 to 73 miles per hour, it is called a tropical storm (storms are given names when they begin to have winds of this speed).

10. The storm becomes a hurricane when there are sustained winds of over 73 miles per hour.

11. When a hurricane travels over land or cold water, its energy source (warm water) is gone and the storm weakens, quickly dying.

Extreme Weather Facts...

Hurricanes are the most destructive natural weather occurrences on Earth.

Extreme Weather Facts...

Hurricanes can cause billions of dollars worth of property damage ever year to man-made fixtures as well as to natural surroundings such as trees and shrubbery. These storms can also change an area's landscape; resulting in hills, roads and trails to wash away.

Extreme Weather Facts...

In 2005 Hurricane Katrina killed over 1800 people in the United States and caused around $80 billion dollars worth of property damage. The city of New Orleans was hit particularly hard with levee breaches leading to around 80% of the city being flooded.

Extreme Weather Facts…

Hurricanes have led to the death of around 2 million people over the last 200 years.

Extreme Weather Facts...

A hurricane that occurred in Bangladesh in 1970, took away the live of one million people. This hurricane is supposedly the worst tornado, in terms of loss of life.

Extreme Weather Facts...

Typhoon Haiyan, known in the Philippines as Typhoon Yolanda, was one of the strongest tropical cyclones ever recorded, which devastated portions of Southeast Asia, particularly the Philippines, on November 8, 2013. It is the deadliest Philippine typhoon on record, killing at least 6,300 people in that country alone. Haiyan is also the strongest storm recorded at landfall, and unofficially the strongest typhoon ever recorded in terms of wind speed. As of January 2014, bodies were still being found.

Extreme Weather Facts...

Hurricanes mostly occur from June 1 to November 30 when seas are the warmest, forming a conducive weather for the hurricanes to build up.

Extreme Weather Facts...

The eye of a hurricane can be anywhere from 2 miles (3.2 kilometres) in diameter to over 200 miles (320 kilometres) but they are usually around 30 miles (48 kilometres).

Extreme Weather Facts…

As well as violent winds and heavy rain, hurricanes can also create tornadoes, high waves and widespread flooding. Coastal regions are most at danger from hurricanes.

Extreme Weather Facts...

Storm surges are frequently the most devastating element of a hurricane. As a hurricane's winds spiral around and around the storm, they push water into a mound at the storm's center. This mound of water becomes dangerous when the storm reaches land because it causes flooding along the coast.

Extreme Weather Facts...

In storm surges the water piles up, unable to escape anywhere but on land as the storm carries it landward. A hurricane will cause more storm surge in areas where the ocean floor slopes gradually. This causes major flooding.

Extreme Weather Facts…

Many people die in hurricanes because of the rising sea water walls that enter the mainland instantly killing people.

Extreme Weather Facts...

The first person to give names to hurricanes was a weather forecaster from Australia named C. Wragge in 1900s. Hurricanes have male and female names, but at one point only female names were used.

Extreme Weather Facts...

Hurricanes are categorized into 5 types, depending upon their wind speed and their capacity to cause damage. The wind speed of the 5 categories are as follows.

Category 1-   74 to 95 miles per hour

Category 2-   96-110 miles per hour

Category 3-   111-130 miles per hour

Category 4-   131-155 miles per hour

Category 5-   Most dangerous. Above 155 miles per hour.

Extreme Weather Facts...

A tornado is a rapidly spinning tube of air that touches both the ground and a cloud above. Tornadoes are sometimes called twisters.

Extreme Weather Facts...

The Fujita Scale is a common way of measuring the strength of tornadoes. The scale ranges from F0 tornadoes that cause minimal damage through to F5 tornadoes which cause massive damage.

Extreme Weather Facts…

Most tornadoes have wind speeds less than 100 miles per hour (161 kilometres per hour). Extreme tornadoes can reach wind speeds of over 300 miles per hour (483 kilometres per hour). Extreme tornadoes can travel much further, sometimes over 100 miles (161 kilometres).

Extreme Weather Facts…

The Tri-State Tornado that travelled through parts of Missouri, Illinois and Indiana in 1925 left a path of destruction over 219 miles (352 kilometres) long. The Tri-State Tornado was the deadliest tornado in US history, killing 695 people.

Hurricane and Tornado Safety Tips

1. Have a disaster plan plan ready.

2. Board up windows and bring in outdoor objects that could blow away.

3. Make sure you know which county or parish you live in and know where all the evacuation routes are.

4. Prepare a disaster supplies kit for your home and car. Include a first aid kit, canned food and a can opener, bottled water, battery-operated radio, flashlight, protective clothing and written instructions on how to turn off electricity, gas, and water.

5. Have a NOAA weather radio handy with plenty of batteries, so you can listen to storm advisories.

6. Have some cash handy as well, because following a hurricane, banks and ATMs may be temporarily closed. Make sure your car is filled with gasoline.

During a Hurricane or Tornado:

1. Stay away from low-lying and flood prone areas.

2. Always stay indoors during a hurricane, because strong winds will blow things around.

3. Leave mobile homes and to go to a shelter.

4. If your home isn't on higher ground, go to a shelter.

5. If emergency managers say to evacuate, then do so immediately.

6. Stay indoors until it is safe to come out.

Made in the USA
San Bernardino, CA
10 October 2017